CONTENTS

JAPAN: PAST AND PRESENT

The archipelago country

Japan is an **archipelago** or group of islands. Although over 4000 islands are actually owned by Japan, most of the country is made up of only four big, closely grouped islands. These are named Hokkaido, Honshu, Shikoku and Kyushu. The Pacific Ocean lies to the east. To the west, Japan is separated from China by the Sea of Japan.

The long chain of Ryukyu Islands stretch far to the south, between the Pacific Ocean and the East China Sea.

Together, all the islands sweep in a gentle curve for a distance of about 3500 kilometres. Put together, its overall size is 378,000 square kilometres, which makes it slightly larger than Germany.

The Hiroshima memorial.
- *The conserved remains of a building that was destroyed on 6 August 1945 when an atomic bomb was dropped on Japan by the USA.*
- *The ruin is a reminder of the horrors of war and nuclear weapons.*

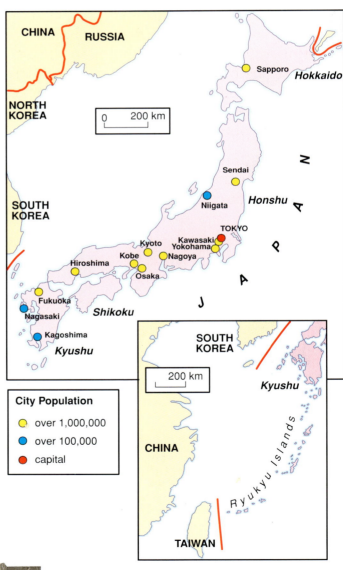

City Population
- over 1,000,000
- over 100,000
- capital

Japan

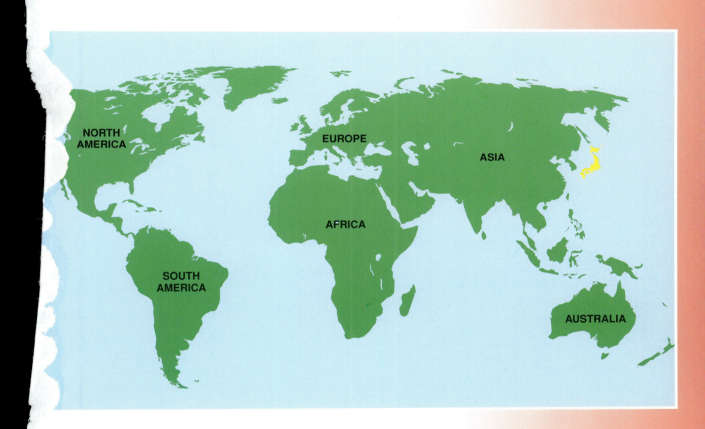

NORTH
AMERICA

EUROPE

ASIA

AFRICA

SOUTH
AMERICA

AUSTRALIA

Fred Martin

Heinemann
LIBRARY

First published in Great Britain by Heinemann Library
Halley Court, Jordan Hill, Oxford OX2 8EJ
a division of Reed Educational and Professional Publishing Ltd

OXFORD FLORENCE PRAGUE MADRID ATHENS
MELBOURNE AUCKLAND KUALA LUMPUR SINGAPORE TOKYO
IBADAN NAIROBI KAMPALA JOHANNESBURG GABORONE
PORTSMOUTH NH CHICAGO MEXICO CITY SAO PAULO

Designed by AMR
Illustrations by Art Construction
Printed and bound in Italy by L.E.G.O.

02 01 00 99 98
10 9 8 7 6 5 4 3 2 1

ISBN 0 431 01357 8
This title is also available in a hardback library edition (ISBN 0 431 01356 X).

British Library Cataloguing in Publication Data

Martin, Fred, 1948-
Next Stop Japan
1. Japan – Geography – Juvenile literature
I.Title II.Japan
915.2

Acknowledgements
The Publishers would like to thank the following for permission to reproduce photographs:
J Allan Cash Ltd, pp.10, 19, 24; Colorific! H. Aga p.25, B. Martin p.8, H. Sautter p.23; Robert Harding Picture Library Ltd p.29; Trip: Trip pp.12, 13, 14, 16, 17, 21, Art Directors p.26, J. Dakers p.6, J. Holmes p.15, T. Morse pp.27-8, P. Rauter pp.18, 22, C. Rennie pp.4, 5, 9, 11, A. Tovy pp.6, 22.

Cover photograph reproduced with permission of Zefa Picture Library (UK) Ltd.

Our thanks to Clare Doran for her comments in the preparation of this book.

Every effort has been made to contact holders of any material reproduced in this book. Any omissions will be rectified in subsequent printings if notice is given to the Publisher.

In the past

Japan has an ancient civilization. From 1637, the rulers of Japan, called *Shoguns,* tried to stop any contact with other countries. In 1854, the USA used warships to force Japan to trade with other countries. After this, Japan quickly became a modern industrial country.

20th-century Japan

Japan fought against Britain and the USA in World War II but surrendered in 1945 after atomic bombs destroyed the cities of Hiroshima and Nagasaki. After the war, Japan was controlled for a short time by the USA. Japan then set up a **democratic** government and continued to build up its industries. Since then, it has become one of the most successful industrial countries in the world. Japan has an emperor as head of state, but like the British monarch, the emperor does not have many powers.

The population of Japan is 125 million, which is almost twice that of the United Kingdom. Most of the people live on the four biggest islands. Eighty per cent of the people live in towns and cities.

The *samurai* were the warriors of the shoguns who fought with swords and followed an extremely strict code of honour. *Samurai* warriors were even prepared to kill themselves if they broke any of their own rules of behaviour.

The Golden Pavilion in its famous ornamental garden in Kyoto.
- *The building is a Buddhist temple that was first built in 1397.*
- *It was rebuilt in 1955 after being destroyed by fire in 1950.*
- *The lake helps to give the scene a sense of peace that is important to followers of Buddhism.*

5

THE NATURAL LANDSCAPE

The devastation after the Kobe earthquake.
- *An earthquake struck the city of Kobe, on Honshu, in January 1995.*
- *About 5000 people were killed.*
- *310,000 people lost their homes because of the quake and the fires that followed.*

Mountains and rivers

There is not much low or flat land on any of Japan's main islands. About 70% of the land is steep and mountainous. The mountain peaks on Honshu often rise to over 3000 metres. Peaks on the other main islands are a bit lower at around 2000 metres on Hokkaido and 1700 metres on Kyushu. The highest peaks are always capped with snow.

Streams and short rivers flow quickly to the sea down the narrow valleys they have carved out. These rivers can quickly overflow and flood when snow melts or during the heavy **monsoon** rains.

Plains and harbours

The land often drops into the sea as steep cliffs. There are some narrow stretches of flat land along the coast. The largest is the Kanto plain on Honshu. There are some wide and deep natural harbours, especially on the eastern side of Japan. Tokyo Bay is one of the finest of these.

A typical Japanese postcard view.
- *Mount Fuji is a dormant volcano with a permanent cap of snow and ice.*
- *The train is Japan's high-speed 'bullet' train.*
- *Rice is growing in the fields.*

Natural hazards

Japan's islands are above a line where two great slabs of the Earth's **crust** meet. These slabs are called **plates**. One plate to the east is slowly moving towards a plate in the west. As they meet, the eastern Pacific plate dips down under the Asian plate. The edge of the plate is melted in the Earth's hot interior. The melted pieces force their way to the surface as molten **lava**. This is what makes volcanoes.

Many of Japan's highest mountains, such as Mount Fuji, are **volcanic cones**. At least 60 of these are still **active volcanoes**. Mount Sakurajima on Kyushu still erupts, covering the city of Kagoshima in ash. Lava comes from more violent eruptions. Some of the smaller islands are the tips of volcanoes that have grown up from the ocean bed.

Moving plates also cause **earthquakes**. There are thousands of small earthquakes every year in Japan and there is a major earthquake from time to time.

Mount Fuji is an important symbol for the Japanese. At 3776 metres it is their highest mountain, a volcanic cone that last erupted in 1707. It has a sacred Shinto shrine on the top.

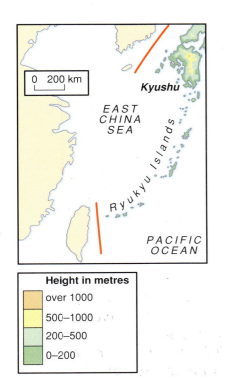

CLIMATE, VEGETATION AND WILDLIFE

Seasons and colour

Each season brings its own colours to the Japanese landscape. Spring is a time when bright red and pink tree blossoms come out. In autumn, leaves turn to yellow and gold. In winter, people in some places can expect thick falls of snow, especially in the northern islands. This is because very cold winds blow out from Siberia to the west. But the most southerly of Japan's islands are never cold. They are near the Tropic of Cancer and stay warm in winter.

Monsoons and typhoons

With the exception of Hokkaido, most of Japan has a **monsoon** climate. This means the wind blows from two main directions at different times of the year. There is a rainy season when the wind blows in warm wet air from the Pacific Ocean in the east. These are called the plum rains.

By September, the weather starts to become cooler. This is a dangerous time when **typhoons** may strike. A typhoon is another name for a **hurricane**.

A sea of umbrellas.
- *There is a wet monsoon season over most of Japan from June to September.*
- *There is heavy rain on most days during this season.*

The Japanese landscape.
- *Most of Japan is mountainous with steep slopes and fast-flowing rivers.*
- *Trees cover land that is too steep for farming.*
- *Tourists are taking a cable car to see Mount Fuji.*

Plants and wildlife

The vegetation in Japan depends on **latitude** and also on height. Tropical trees and bushes grow on the most southerly islands.

On the four main islands, the type of vegetation changes as you go higher up the mountains. At sea level, there are cedar trees that are up to 2000 years old. Above this, there are forests of **deciduous trees** such as beech and oak. At about 2000 metres, there are fir trees. Even higher there are small shrubs, mosses and some flowers. In some areas natural vegetation has been cleared for farming, especially in the lower land.

There are many types of birds, reptiles and mammals living in the wild. There is a giant Japanese **salamander** that grows up to 1.5 metres long. There are macaque monkeys, racoon dogs and venomous snakes. Bears, deer and foxes all live in the mountain forests.

There is an annual snow festival in the city of Sapporo on the northern island of Hokkaido. Giant figures are carved out of ice. You can expect to see sculptures of almost anything, from an octopus to a temple!

TOWNS AND CITIES

A busy street scene in the Akihabara shopping district of Tokyo.
- *A railway line runs over the road to make the most of space.*
- *There are signs in both Japanese and English.*

Crowded cities

Towns and cities in Japan are some of the world's most crowded places. There are 135 towns and cities with a population of over 100,000 people. Eleven of these contain over 1 million people. In the UK, there are 67 cities with over 100,000 people and only 4 with over 1 million. However, Japan does have almost twice as many people as the UK.

Space in Japanese cities is so short that there is a special sunshine **tax**. This has to be paid if a new building blocks out sunlight on nearby buildings. Homes are usually very small. Everything has to be carefully packed inside each room to make the best possible use of the space available.

Tokyo is the biggest city in Japan and is its **capital city**. About 12 million people live in Tokyo. This makes it one of the world's most highly populated cities. The name Tokyo means 'the eastern capital' in Japanese.

Cities at risk

Tokyo has been almost destroyed twice this century. In 1923, an earthquake flattened thousands of buildings killing about 110,000 people. There is a reminder of this each year when there is an earthquake drill for everyone in Tokyo. The city was then bombed and burnt during World War II. Very few of the city's original wooden houses have survived.

After World War II, cities in Japan were rebuilt from concrete, steel and glass. These buildings should survive an earthquake, but nobody can tell until it happens. Another threat is from giant waves called *tsunamis*. They are caused by an earthquake on the ocean bed which sends a giant wall of water crashing onto the shore.

Coastal towns

Most of Japan's towns and cities are in the narrow flat spaces between the mountains and the sea. These are usually industrial towns and ports, such as Yokohoma, Nagoya and Osaka. Some cities are so short of land that the sea has been filled in with rock to provide more space for buildings. The Kansai International Airport, opened in 1994, was built on land reclaimed from the sea near Osaka.

The average amount of open space for each person in Tokyo is only 2.7 square metres. In London, the average amount of open space is 30 square metres, more than ten times more.

The city of Nagasaki on the island of Kyushu.
- *About 450,000 people live in Nagasaki.*
- *Buildings are crowded onto the small amount of flat land between the mountains and the coast.*
- *The Peace Park in Nagasaki reminds people of the atomic bomb that destroyed the city in 1945.*

LIVING IN TOKYO

The Shishido family home

The Shishido family live in the Chiba prefecture (district) on the edge of Tokyo. The family members are Hajime the father, Junko the mother, their daughter Emi, son Yuta, grandfather Tadao and grandmother Fumi.

The family house is a modern two-storey building with five main rooms. There is not enough land to have a garden. At night, all the main living rooms are made into bedrooms.

The Shishido family home.
- *The family are lucky to have a home as big as this in Tokyo.*

The daily routine

Hajime is 40 years old. At 7.00 am, he goes to his work in a publishing company. The journey takes about an hour by train. He comes home in the evening, sometimes as late as 9.00 pm.

Junko is also 40 years old. She gets up at 6.00 am. Breakfast is usually either rice, fish, eggs, *miso* soup or salads. Between 8.30 am and 2.00 pm she works in a shop that makes lunches. After work, she may go to the supermarket, do some housework and then prepare the evening meal. The family like eating *sushi*, steak or Chinese meals.

Eating an evening meal.
- *During the week, Hajime is not usually at home for the evening meal.*

Yuta and his mother set off for school.
• He has two more years before he starts secondary school.

Tadao is 70 years old and Fumi is 69 years old. They mostly stay at home helping with the housework. It is a tradition in Japan that parents live with their children, even when they are grown-up.

All work and some play

Emi is 13 years old and is in the first year of the junior high school. She goes to school early for badminton club – at 6.30 am and often gets back at 6.00 pm. Like many other children, she goes to a private school in the evenings, where she does extra studies for her examinations. She does not come home again until after 10.00 pm.

Shopping in the local supermarket.
• The supermarkets are very careful with fresh produce. They even wrap their carrots in individual plastic bags!

Yuta is aged ten and is in the fourth grade of his primary school. He leaves for school at 7.00 am and returns at 3.00 pm. His hobbies are swimming and football. He also learns *Shuji* (Japanese handwriting) and how to use an **abacus**.

Hajime on his way to the office.
• *The Tokyo underground is the quickest way to get to work.*

FARMING LANDSCAPES

Lack of land

The climate over most of Japan is ideal for growing many types of food. However, only about 14% of the land can be farmed. Most of the rest is too steep, too high, or is used for buildings and roads.

The shortage of farm land is one reason why the average size of farms is very small. At 1.4 hectares, most farms are about the size of three football pitches. Farmers make the most of every piece of land by clearing stones, weeding and by using chemical **fertilizers**. Steep slopes are cut into steps called **terraces** to help give more flat space.

Crops and family farms

Rice is one of the main crops. Rice has to be under water for part of the time it is growing. This means that the fields have to be **irrigated**. Low mud walls are built around each small field to hold the water in. Farmers also use these walls to walk from field to field.

Rice growing with banks of soil separating the fields.
- *Rice must grow in water taken from a nearby river.*
- *There are special types of machinery which work in Japan's small muddy fields.*
- *Only 7% of people in Japan work in farming.*

Fishermen unloading their catch at a fishing port on the island of Hokkaido.
- *Most of the boats are small and do not go far from the land.*
- *Fresh fish is taken to be sold in city markets.*

Most farmers use small tractors and mechanical harvesters. These machines have to be small to fit into the fields. Farmers also rear pigs and grow vegetables such as beans and cabbages.

Most farms are small family businesses. The whole family, including the children, has to help with the work. In the past, the eldest son was expected to take over the family farm. However, not as many people want to work in farming any more. Jobs in the city can be better paid, less mucky and take less physical effort.

Fishing for food

There are about 270,000 fishing boats in Japan. Most are small boats that work close to the shore. There are also some **fish farms** where fish are specially reared.

In spite of its lack of farm land, Japan produces about 60% of all the food it needs (the UK produces 72% of the food it needs). In basic foods, such as rice, potatoes and vegetables, almost everything that is needed is grown in Japan.

LIVING IN THE COUNTRY

Seiji and Mariko's home

The Yonezumi family live in the Mie district near Nabari City. This area is a $1\frac{1}{2}$ hour train journey from Osaka. It is about 350 km south-west of Tokyo, on the island of Honshu. The Mie district is a country area where some people still live and work on farms.

There are seven people in the Yonezumi family. They live together in a house built from traditional local materials such as wood and straw. Inside, the house is very comfortable with all the conveniences of a modern home.

Six members of the Yonezumi family.
- *The house is a traditional farmhouse.*
- *Mostly local materials were used to build the house.*

Somebody is missing from the photo of the family home. This is because Seiji [say-jee], the father, is at his work. During the week, he leaves to go to work in an office at 6.30 am, and returns at 8.00 pm. It takes him an hour to get to work on his motorbike. His wife Mariko gets up at 6.00 am. After breakfast and when the children have gone to school, she goes to a part-time job for most of the day.

The Yonezumi family eating breakfast.
- *Most of the food is eaten from small bowls using chopsticks.*
- *Everyone sits on the floor for breakfast by tradition, though they often sit on chairs for the evening meal.*

Grandmother Kiyo at work on the farm.
- *She is tending a plot of vegetables.*
- *Can you recognize some of the vegetables?*

The Yonezumi children

There are three children in the Yonezumi family. The oldest is Tomoaki. He is twelve years old, so he is in the sixth grade at primary school. He sets off at 7.30 am. All the local children meet to walk the $2\frac{1}{2}$ km to school. On Friday, Tomoaki goes to a private school after his normal day at school. This is so he can learn more and do well in the exams that will get him into a good secondary school.

Masataka is nine years old, so he is still in the third grade. The youngest son is Naochika, who is six years old. He goes to the kindergarten school. At home, the children enjoy watching television and playing computer games. They play football and games outside with the other local children when there is time.

Meet the grandparents

Grandfather Toshikazu is 65 years old, and Grandmother Kiyo is 67 year old. They do most of the farm work in spite of their age. Seiji and Mariko both prefer to do other types of work.

In modern Japan, it is hard to earn enough out of a small amount of farmland. The Japanese tradition of passing the farm down to the eldest son is one that many eldest sons do not want to follow.

Tomoaki walks to school every morning.
- *The yellow cap is part of Tomoaki's school uniform.*

WHAT'S IN JAPANESE SHOPS?

Standard of living

Many people in Japan earn a good wage and want to buy good quality food, clothes and other goods. Small shops, department stores, supermarkets and traditional street markets are all part of the life of every town and city in Japan.

Markets and *supas*

Some farmers drive their vegetables and other produce to the city markets every day. Fish are often sold live out of a water tank to prove to the customer that they are fresh. Rice is often bought from special shops. This is because it is such an important part of the diet.

Bread is not a traditional food in Japan, although some people now eat bread at certain meals in place of rice.

There are modern supermarkets in Japan. The word *supa* is used to describe a supermarket. Supermarkets are becoming more popular as more women go out to work. They stock up for the week in a supermarket, as they no longer have the time to buy the shopping every day from small shops and local markets.

Selling root vegetables at a market stall.
- *People in Japan like to buy fresh food.*
- *Onions, cabbages, soya beans and sweet potatoes are among the vegetables sold from market stalls.*

Shops in Japan sell many types of electrical goods that are made in Japan.

- *Electrical goods made by manufacturers such as Toshiba are sold all over the world.*

Consumer goods

Goods such as clothes and electrical equipment are likely to be bought in a department store in the city centre. Most Japanese homes have a colour television set, computer, microwave, rice boiler and other electrical gadgets. Most people also have a traditional low table with heating beneath called a *kotatsu*. This is useful in winter when it becomes very cold.

People buy and wear western clothes such as jeans and suits, especially in the cities. Only rich women can afford the traditional Japanese *kimono*, a long loose robe tied with a sash. It takes about 20 minutes to put on a *kimono*. Traditional clothes are usually kept for special occasions such as weddings and other religious or family celebrations.

Japanese shoppers may soon be able to buy the world's first television sets to hang from the wall rather like paintings. These are currently being developed by Japan's high-tech electronics companies.

JAPANESE COOKING

Rice and vegetables

Rice is eaten with most meals in Japan. In Japanese, the word used for rice is the same as the word for food. Rice is usually served in a separate bowl. Sometimes it is served mixed with a beaten raw egg. Another popular way to eat rice is in the form of crackers. *Sake* [sar-keh] is a type of wine made from fermented rice juice.

Vegetables are also part of most meals. Most people in Japan eat very little meat because it is expensive and not part of their traditional diet. Vegetables can be pickled or stir-fried in a pan. Some dishes, such as *miso* soup, are made from edible seaweed and soya bean paste.

Soya beans are cooked like vegetables or made into soya sauce, to be sprinkled over food. Soya beans are also made into *tofu* by straining soya milk from the beans and adding some lemon. This makes the milk change into a curd. *Tofu* is sold either fresh or dried.

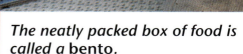

The neatly packed box of food is called a bento.
- *Most of the food is rice, but it has different flavours, with delicate samples of seaweed, egg or pickled vegetables.*
- *Meals are usually eaten with chopsticks.*

A fish market in Tokyo.
- A tuna fish is being cut up.
- Both raw and cooked fish is eaten in Japan.

Fish and meat

The Japanese eat a lot of fish and seafood, prepared in many different ways. *Sushi* chefs cut raw fish into small cubes or slices and serve it with rice mixed with vinegar, sugar and salt. Fish is also eaten coated with batter and fried with vegetables. This is called *tempura*.

Sukiyaki is a dish made with thinly cut strips of beef, noodles, vegetables, bamboo shoots, *tofu* and chrysanthemum leaves. This is then cooked on a little electric cooker or gas ring burner.

Looking good

A Japanese meal would not be right if it did not look as good as it tasted. Vegetables and fish may be cut to look like flowers. Colours are often bright and chosen to go well together. Each small portion is laid out to look its best on the plate.

Special licensed chefs have to be very careful when cutting up a blowfish. The blowfish has a poison that has to be removed before it can be eaten. The blowfish is so dangerous that it kills about five people every year!

MADE IN JAPAN

Famous names

There will be at least one thing made by a Japanese company in most of our homes. This could be a Nissan or Toyota car or something electrical such as a Hitachi television or video, a Sharp pocket calculator or a Sony CD player. Some of these things are made in the UK by Japanese companies. Others are made in Japan and **exported**. Success at making goods and selling them abroad is what has given Japan such a strong **economy**.

Car-making companies such as Toyota, Nissan and Subaru are known all over the world. Suzuki and Honda are world leaders in making motorbikes. These companies make and export products that are usually cheaper than other makes. In the factories, inspectors constantly check the work and the quality of the parts. Robots are used in production to keep the standard of each product to the same high quality and to keep the costs down.

Industries of all kinds have helped make Japan a successful economy.
- *Metals are smelted and oil is refined to give raw materials and energy.*
- *Air pollution from factories and from vehicles can be a problem in many Japanese cities.*

Raw materials

The success of industries in Japan is a little surprising. There are almost no **raw materials**, such as iron ore, in Japan and no oil or other types of **fossil fuel**. All of these things have to be **imported**. It is hard to pay the cost of imported goods and still make products to sell at a price that buyers can afford.

In spite of this, more steel is made in Japan than in almost any other country. It is also the largest ship producer in the world. More plastics and other products, such as petrol, that come from oil are made in Japan than in any other country.

Company workers

In the large Japanese companies, workers often stay with the same company from the day they start work until the day they retire. Workers are helped with buying homes, holidays and with health care. They do their jobs in teams and share in making decisions about how improvements could be made. **Strikes** are rare.

However, the tradition of staying loyal to one company for the whole of your working life is changing. Younger workers want the freedom to move between companies to get more experience and so they can be promoted more quickly. Even so, working hard is one Japanese tradition that is still as important as ever.

More cars are made in Japan than in any other country. Almost one car in every three in the world is made in Japan. Just under 8 million cars are made in Japan each year.

A motor car assembly line.
- *Much of the work is done by robots and other machines.*
- *The work is carefully checked by teams of workers.*

TRANSPORT AND TRAVEL

Railways and 'bullet trains'

The Shinkansen 'bullet train' travels at a top speed of 270 kilometres per hour. This is actually much slower than a real bullet, but it is the fastest way to travel on land in Japan. It takes only $2\frac{1}{2}$ hours to travel the 550 kilometres between Tokyo and Osaka. This is the same distance as between London and Edinburgh, a journey which takes 4 hours by train. Fast trains also link most of the other cities in Japan.

Commuters often travel by local trains for several hours before arriving in the big cities to work every day. In Tokyo, station staff help cram in more passengers by pushing them onto the trains. There is so little space in the cities that some rail lines pass through the sides of buildings. **Monorails** have been built to make more space for travelling. Ten of the main cities have underground rail systems.

Roads, pavements and railways in the cities are built on different levels to make the best use of space.
- *Traffic congestion is a problem in the cities.*
- *Air pollution caused by vehicles is also a problem.*

Roads and fumes

Motorways such as the Tomei and Meishin **expressways** link all the main cities. Getting through the mountains can sometimes be a problem. The 300-kilometre expressway between Tokyo and Niigata includes a tunnel through mountains almost 11 kilometres long.

Motorways have been built through the cities to try to keep traffic moving in areas where there are daily traffic jams. Cyclists and pedestrians often wear face masks in the cities to protect themselves from car fumes. People can buy oxygen from canisters on the roadsides.

Islands and aircraft

Travelling between Japan's many islands used to be difficult. Now there are bridges and tunnels between them. The world's longest tunnel links Honshu with Hokkaido. This is the Seikan rail tunnel and it is almost 54 kilometres long. A road tunnel is being built under Tokyo harbour to link the city with towns and villages on the other side of the large bay.

The main cities are also linked by regular air services. This is the only practical way for passengers to get to Japan's most southerly islands such as Okinawa. The flight from Tokyo takes $2\frac{1}{2}$ hours. The same journey takes 60 hours by boat.

An incredible 2.8 million passengers pass through Tokyo's Shinjuku railway station every day.

The Tokyo subway is very crowded as people travel to and from work.
* *Passengers are squeezed into the train by a station worker wearing a uniform and white gloves.*

LEISURE AND SPORT

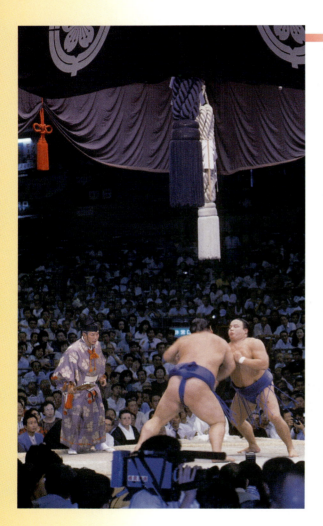

Sumo wrestling is a popular spectator sport in Japan.
- *Most Sumo wrestlers are men but there are also some women Sumo wrestlers.*
- *This type of wrestling may become an Olympic sport.*

Ancient and modern

Many things people do in Japan are a mixture of the old and the new. This is also true for what people do in their leisure time.

Japan is where several types of self-defence called **martial arts** began. *Judo* and *kendo* are two of the most popular of these. *Judo* is fought by throwing an opponent to the ground. *Kendo* is fought like a sword fight but using sticks instead of swords. *Sumo* wrestlers battle to throw each other out of a ring. The ceremony before the fight usually lasts longer than the fight itself!

Other sports, such as baseball, basketball and golf, have become popular. Playing golf is very expensive and there are not many golf clubs because there is so little land. A game on a golf course needs to be booked at least a month in advance. Most golfers practise on a driving range, and some even use **Virtual Reality** to perfect their swing!

A soccer league was started in 1992 and is already a success. Skiing and snow boarding make use of the mountain landscapes and heavy snowfalls. The winter Olympic Games are due to be held in Japan in 1998.

This family is visiting a local park to see the blossoms in spring.
* *About 1 in 3 of all Japanese people regularly visit parks in their spare time.*

Origami and the Internet

Origami is a traditional hobby that is still practised. This involves the intricate folding of paper to make the shapes of animals and other objects. *Ikebana* is the art of arranging flowers. About 15 million people in Japan go to classes to learn how to do *Ikebana*.

Many children and adults are now more interested in electronic forms of entertainment. These include playing video games and using their computers to make contact with people around the world on the **Internet**.

A day out

Water is important to the Japanese for enjoyment, to keep clean and for religious reasons. Children often learn to swim in their school swimming pool. For adults, taking a bath in hot water springs is a popular way to relax. The hot volcanic rocks in Japan heat up underground water in places such as Beppu, in Kyushu.

Days out might be spent in a park looking at the tree blossoms or visiting one of the ancient **Shinto** or **Buddhist** temples.

Karaoke **has become a popular type of entertainment in many countries. People sing in front of their friends to the backing of taped music.** *Karaoke* **began in Japan. The Japanese word** *Karaoke* **means 'an empty orchestra'.**

CUSTOMS AND ARTS

Public holidays

There are fifteen public holiday days in Japan. This is far more than in most other countries. These days include 'Health Sports Day', 'Children's Day', 'Respect for the Aged Day' and the 'Birthday of the Emperor'. There are also days to celebrate the Spring and Autumn equinoxes, the times of year when day and night are of equal length. The main celebration is at New Year. People visit **Shinto** shrines and eat noodles as a sign of long life. In August, the spirits of the dead are supposed to pay a visit to their relatives for three days.

Religion and festivals

Shinto and **Buddhism** are the two main beliefs in Japan. Many people in Japan consider themselves to be both Buddhist and Shintoist so they go to ceremonies and festivals for both religions. Marriages are likely to be in a Shinto shrine but funerals might take place at a Buddhist temple.

Festivals are a time of colour, decoration and enjoyment. The New Year festival is the most important national festival when families get together. Flags and banners in the shape of a fish called a carp are flown on Children's Day. At the Aoi festival in Kyoto, people dress in the traditional clothes worn long ago at the ancient emperor's court.

The Hadaka festival in Osaka.
- *The name of this festival means 'naked'.*
- *The festival is held in winter so men can show how brave they are.*

The Japanese tea ceremony.
- *The* **Geisha** *women are highly trained in all the arts and are highly cultured and respected. One of the ceremonies they perform so well is the tea ceremony, which dates back at least 800 years.*

Tea and theatre

The Japanese tea ceremony called *chanoyu* first came from Buddhist monks. They used it to help them **meditate**. The tea leaves are ground to a fine green powder, then water is added and briskly stirred. The ceremony can last for up to four hours.

Traditional *Noh* and *Kabuki* plays tell stories about ancient battles and heroes. They are performed wearing elaborate costumes and painted masks. There are also *bunraku* plays that use big puppets worked by up to three people.

Haiku is a kind of poem, usually about nature, which discusses the truths about life. They are written in only 3 lines. Modern *haiku* poets are now writing about more up-to-date issues.

Of course, people also enjoy watching films and other drama on television and in the cinema. There is traditional music in Japan but people are also interested in western classical music and pop music.

The Suzuki method of learning to play the violin was invented by Dr. Suzuki in Japan. Children as young as three learn by copying their teacher and playing from memory.

JAPAN FACTFILE

Area 378,000 square km
Highest point Mount Fuji 3776m

Climate

	January temp.	July temp.	Total annual rainfall
Tokyo	4°C	25°C	1563 mm

Population 125 million
Population density 330 people per square km

Life expectancy
Female 83 years
Male 77 years

Capital city Tokyo

Population of the main cities (in millions)

Tokyo	11.9
Yokohama	3.2
Osaka	2.6
Nagoya	2.2
Sapporo	1.7
Kobe	1.5
Kyoto	1.4
Fukuoka	1.2
Kawasaki	1.2
Hiroshima	1.1

Land use

Forest	67%
Farming	14%
Other	19%

Employment

Services	69%
Industry	24%
Farming	7%

Main imports
Oil and other mineral fuels
Machinery and transport equipment
Manufactured goods
Raw materials
Food

Main exports
Machinery and transport equipment
Manufactured goods (electrical goods, cameras)
Chemicals

Language

Japanese	99%
Other	1%

Religions

Shintoist	93%
Buddhist	74%
Christian	1%

Note: Many Japanese people are both Shintoists and Buddhists.

Money
The Japanese yen

Wealth $31,490
(The total value of what is produced by the country in one year, divided by its population and converted into US dollars).

GLOSSARY

abacus a counting frame, helping people to add, subtract and multiply

active volcano a volcano that is still likely to erupt

archipelago a group of islands

Buddhism a world religion, founded in India in the 5th century BC

capital city the city where a country has its government

commuter a person who regularly travels a long way to work

crust the thin, hard outer layer of the Earth

deciduous trees trees that shed their leaves at the end of the growing season

democratic a political system that gives equal power and rights to the people

earthquake violent shaking of the ground

economy the creation and management of the wealth of a country based on the value of its exports and imports

exports goods sent out of a country to be sold to other countries

expressways motorways

fertilizer a substance added to soil to make it more fertile

fish farm an enclosed area where fish are reared

fossil fuel fuels such as oil, coal and gas, produced from decayed plants and animals

hurricane severe weather with high winds and heavy rain

imports goods brought into a country to be sold there

Internet a huge computer network which connects millions of people around the world

irrigation a watering system set up to water the land

latitude imaginary lines of measurement around the Earth which run parallel to the Equator

lava molten rock that flows out of a volcano

martial arts sports where people fight each other with their hands or weapons

meditate concentrate the mind on a single purpose, usually spiritual

monorails trains that run on a single overhead rail

monsoon a type of climate where the wind blows from two main directions bringing heavy rain at a certain season

plates large sections of the Earth's crust

raw materials the materials needed to make things

salamander an animal related to the newt

Shinto one of the main belief systems in Japan. It includes the worship of ancestors and spirits.

strike when employees stop work to protest about pay or working conditions

tax an amount of money charged to people by the state

terraces steps cut into a hillside to create areas of land which can be farmed

typhoon severe weather with high winds and heavy rain

Virtual Reality an artificial, computer-created world which viewers feel they are part of

volcanic cone the mountain peak made by a volcano

INDEX